101 ways to gross out your friends

BY JULIE HUFFMAN
ILLUSTRATED BY JIM PAILLOT

Quarto is the authority on a wide range of topics.
Quarto educates, entertains, and enriches the lives of our readers—
enthusiasts and lovers of hands-on living.
www.quartoknows.com

Illustrated by Jim Paillot
Written by Julie Huffman

6 Orchard Road, Suite 100
Lake Forest, CA 92630
quartoknows.com
Visit our blogs at quartoknows.com

MIX
Paper from
responsible sources
FSC® C101537

Printed in China
1 3 5 7 9 10 8 6 4 2

INTRODUCTION

Welcome to *101 Ways to Gross Out Your Friends*. I hope you have a tremendous amount of fun reading the disgusting stories, guffawing at the cheesy jokes, and howling with laughter as you complete each activity. Some take a bit of time to complete, and some are super-fast. But they're all designed to **gross out you and your friends!**

The truth is, as a life-long science lover, I've discovered **playing with the gross stuff** is the perfect way to develop a real passion for science. Giggle while making kitty-litter poop, or watch people stand in horror as you eat zombie intestines or gulp down "urine" like there's no tomorrow. **It's all in the name of science.** Biology, chemistry, and physics explain all the marvels of our planet. Study the science in this book, and soon you'll be an expert in all things ooey and gooey. Ready to gross out everyone you know?

TABLE OF CONTENTS

GETTING STARTED

CHOOSING AN ACTIVITY

In this book, you can geek out on grossness with new vocab, fun facts, and jokes to impress your friends. Grossologists can work their way through 1 to 101, or tackle the activities in any order that looks fun. Recipes and activities take more time, but are totally worth it. If you're in the mood for a speed read, there are lots of strange-but-true stories, as well as some that are gross but not true. Your friends won't know the difference.

ASSEMBLING THE INGREDIENTS

Just like when you're cooking or baking, when you're making slimy, gooey gunk, you'll want to assemble everything you're going to need before you start. Ask permission before using mom's best bowls to mix things in. Better yet, enlist her help!

CARE OF SLIMY GOOEY GUNK

Your creations will not last forever. Keep them in airtight plastic storage bags. But even so, when they dry out, mold, or smell worse than they should, get rid of them and make new goo.

DISPOSAL OF SLIMY GOOEY GUNK

No need to call any special governmental agency. Just open the garbage can and toss.

HOUSEHOLD CONCERNS

Sticky substances are not nice to surfaces—they leave a mess. Sometimes they even stain. So lay down a towel or some other "splat mat" to absorb the mess. Remember, cleaning up is a necessary chore if you ever want to be allowed in the kitchen again.

WARNINGS

With some of the recipes you may need an adult accomplice to help out, especially when using the stove. This is gross fun, not clean fun.

A CASE OF ARRESTED DEVELOPMENT

If you've ever been told to grow up, then this book is for you. And yep, there's also a fair amount of redeeming educational value.

GO. DO DISGUSTING THINGS. HAVE FUN!

1

WHAT IS VOMIT?

The scientific term for vomiting is *emesis*— the forceful involuntary expulsion of an individual's stomach contents through the mouth (and sometime the nose).

Vomiting can also be called *throwing up, retching, spewing, puking, ralphing, hurling, upchucking, tossing your cookies,* or plain old *barfing.* It's usually the result of your body responding to an unwanted virus or bacteria, but it can also be the result of too much food, spoiled food, stress, or dizziness. It is your body's way of clearing your stomach. As basic as it seems—you feel sick and say hello to your last meal—vomiting is actually a complicated mechanism involving the brain, nerves, and the muscles in your gastrointestinal track.

2 EXPAND YOUR VOCABULARY

What other words or phrases can you think of to say *vomit*?

There's *bark, blow chunks, chuck, clean house, gag, barf, heave, huey, hurl, launch, lose lunch, puke, ralph, regurgitate, retch, reverse gut, ride the porcelain bus, sneeze cheese, spew, throw up, toss your tacos,* and *upchuck*—just to name a few.

3 STRANGE BUT TRUE!

The internet has claimed for years that astronauts have left bags of vomit on the moon. According to NASA, astronauts did leave an *empty* emesis bag on the moon. These bags are brought along in the event of sickness, but due to limited space (doh!), they had to be left behind.

4 MAKE THEM LAUGH!

Q: What do you call explosive cow vomit?
A: A cud missile!

Q: What do you give a sick lemon?
A: Lemon-aid!

DID YOU KNOW?

5

The only food baby birds can digest is food their mother eats first, then throws up.

6 Cows regurgitate their food and chew it again (hence the phrase "chewing their cud"). It helps cows get the most out of difficult-to-digest foods, including grass.

SPEW-LICIOUS!

GLOW IN THE DARK VOMIT

This gross activity works best in a dark room! It is also a fun surprise to fool guests with.

WHAT YOU'LL NEED
- Bottle of tonic water (the label must say quinine)
- Bucket to fake "spew" into!
- Black light
- Miscellaneous inexpensive glow-in-the-dark toys/gadgets (these, along with the black light, can be found at your nearest party supply store)

Have tonic water poured, hidden, and an empty bucket strategically placed before your guests arrive. Turn on the black light and have them examine the glow-in-the-dark objects, as you explain the science.

THE SCIENCE
Objects that contain phosphors glow, because of the way they convert ultraviolet radiation from the black light into visible light we can see.

HOW TO MAKE IT

Once you have them in the palm of your ultraviolet hand, secretly take a big sip of tonic water, swish it around in your mouth, grab your stomach, groan, and "vomit" into the bucket. Your guests will be simultaneously horrified and then delighted at the beautiful glow of your fake barf. Of course, you should repeat the process a few more times for full effect. The best part? No harm, no foul. If you accidentally swallow some, it's just tonic water! How does it work? Tonic water contains quinine, a compound which naturally fluoresces when exposed to ultraviolet light!

MAKE YOUR OWN BARF
(WITHOUT THROWING UP!)

Leaving a pile of chunky barf somewhere is a surefire way to disgust friends and family.

Use the ingredients below to get started, but be creative—the weirder the better. You can use things like bacon bits, raisins, and pieces of lettuce to add more chunks!

WHAT YOU'LL NEED

- ½ cup water
- 3 packets of unflavored gelatin
- 1 drop of yellow food coloring
- 1 teaspoon white vinegar
- 3 tablespoons light corn syrup
- Uncooked oatmeal
- Fork
- Plastic bag or plate

HOW TO MAKE IT

Microwave the water for 1 minute on high in a microwave-safe bowl. Slowly add the gelatin, and let it sit for 2 to 3 minutes. Stir with a fork until the gelatin is dissolved. Add yellow food coloring, vinegar, and corn syrup. Stir again with a fork. Sprinkle in oatmeal and any other food chunks you want to add. Then spoon the mixture onto a plastic bag or plate until you have the desired amount of barf. Chill in the refrigerator, and when it's firm, peel it off the plastic. Voila! Fake barf!

TIP!

For a creamier version, add ¼ cup cornstarch to your mixture and microwave again for 30 seconds. Stir until you get a pasty substance. If barf is still too watery, microwave for an additional 30 seconds.

9

WHAT IS SNOT?

Whether you sniff, snort, or slurp it, snot or mucus, serves an important biological function!

The average human body produces 1 to 1.5 liters of mucus each day! This sticky, gooey stuff is responsible for catching unwanted germs, so when the body is coming down with a cold, it goes into overdrive to produce more snot in the hopes of getting rid of that virus or bacteria. That's what causes a runny nose! Boogers are simply chunks of mucus that have dried up in the nose. Science has even come up with terms to describe the act of picking your nose. The occasional pick is known as *rhinotillexis*. Chronic nasal mining is called *rhinotillexomania*.

NOSE
CONSTANTLY
RUNNY

CRUSTY,
SNOTTY
FACE

A BOX OF TISSUE HANDY

19

10 STRANGE BUT TRUE!

If the fluid coming from your nose is super clear and seems never-ending, you may want to see an ear, nose, and throat specialist. Cerebrospinal fluid rhinorrhea is a rare condition that results from a small tear near the brain, causing spinal fluid to flow from your body just like a runny nose! *Yeesh.*

11 MAKE THEM LAUGH!

Q: Why do gorillas have large nostrils?
A: Because they have fat fingers.

Q: How do you make a tissue dance?
A: Put a little boogie into it.

Q: What does an elephant keep up its nose?
A: A meter and a half of snot!

Q: Where does your nose go when it gets hungry?
A: Booger King.

Q: What's yellow, gooey, and smells like bananas?
A: Monkey snot.

DID YOU KNOW?

 Humans recycle about a quart of snot a day by swallowing it! *Gulp.*

13 The speed of a sneeze (which is another way your body gets rid of bacteria and viruses) moves at about 100 mph (or 160 kph). Compare that to a running cheetah, which clocks in at 60 mph (or 96 kph)!

DINO SNOT

A hundred million years ago, give or take, dinosaur snot was a valuable all-purpose substance.

CROSS BUT NOT TRUE

Cave people risked their lives for just a few handfuls. They would follow dinosaurs through the jungles, and as snot dripped from the beasts' noses, they would scoop it up and carry it away in baskets. They used it as lip balm and massaged it into their aching muscles. Who says we haven't evolved?

WHAT YOU'LL NEED

- 1 teaspoon Metamucil* (found at the grocery store)
- 1 cup of water
- 1 drop of red food coloring
- 2 drops of blue food coloring

HOW TO MAKE IT

In a microwave-safe bowl, dissolve Metamucil in water. Microwave on high for 4 minutes or just until the mixture looks like it will boil over. Let it rest 1 minute, and repeat until it is the desired consistency. The more you microwave the mixture, the more rubbery it will become. Add food coloring to give your dino snot a prehistoric glow.

THE SCIENCE

Metamucil is made of psyllium husk, which easily absorbs water and swells to form a gelatin-like goo. In water, psyllium forms a colloidal suspension. That means the more you heat it up, the more water will be driven off, leaving you with a lovely snotty concoction.

NOW, WHAT DO YOU DO WITH IT?

- Make up a game with your friends called "Toss the Snot."
- Pretend to sneeze, and let it fly! (Make a green batch for this one.)
- Put it in the fridge, and let it thicken to the consistency of boogers. Then flick it at your little brother or sister.

*Metamucil is an over-the-counter fiber supplement. Although safe to ingest, it is used in this activity for purely scientific, gooey fun. Don't eat your homemade snot.

15

WHAT IS URINE?

Urine is produced by the kidneys as they filter waste from our blood and monitor the balance of water in our bodies. It's created when the body turns proteins into energy and produces ammonia. The ammonia combines with carbon dioxide in the liver to produce urea and water, or urine.

Whether you have to wee, tinkle, pee, take a leak, use the potty, or take a wiz, everyone has to urinate. Usually urine ranges from a light to dark yellow color, depending on the amount of water in it. It can turn neon bright if you eat a lot of vitamin B. Eating lots of beets, rhubarb, or blackberries can turn it a reddish brown.

FIXATED ON
NEED TO
RELIEVE ONESELF

SAMPLE

EMPTY BLADDER

CROSSED LEGS

27

16 STRANGE BUT TRUE!

Do you feel better about swimming in a pool when it smells strongly of chlorine? For years, people have been told that the strong smell and the burning in our eyes is a result of chlorine meant to keep pools super clean. The truth? The burning and the strong odor are caused by chlorine bonding to the urine and sweat in pools. A 2013 study from the United States Center for Disease Control and Prevention even found e. coli, "a marker for fecal contamination," in 58 percent of pools studied. Now everybody in!

17 MAKE THEM LAUGH!

Q: If you are American in the kitchen, what are you in the bathroom?
A: European.

Q: Why can't you hear a pterodactyl going to the bathroom?
A: Because the p is silent.

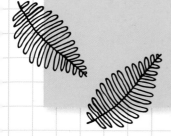

29

DID YOU KNOW?

18

The human bladder can hold about the same amount of liquid as a can of soda.

19

Scientists now have the ability to purify urine. Astronaut Scott Kelly drank over 700 liters of recycled sweat and urine during his year on the International Space Station!

20

SEWER LICE

One dark and rainy night, I discovered little slimy, slithery critters in a puddle under a sewer pipe.

I had read about the creatures, but believed them to be a myth. I scooped them in a container and ran home to learn they were much more. They were the legendary sewer lice!

THE SCIENCE

The raisins move up and down in the beverage because of carbon dioxide (CO_2)! The raisins are denser than the liquid, so they sink. Then CO_2 from the beverage collects on the raisins' surface, making them more buoyant and causing them to rise. When they reach the surface, the CO_2 bubbles pop, causing the process to start all over again.

The lice are most active when those observing them are completely silent. Catch the plumpest one you can to find out!

WHAT YOU'LL NEED

- 1 yellow, carbonated beverage
- Pack of raisins
- Beaker (or other clear container)

HOW TO MAKE IT

Gather your bubbly beverage and some raisins, and place them together in a beaker (or other clear container).

NOW, WHAT DO YOU DO WITH IT?

Show the lice to all your fellow science enthusiasts! Make sure to lure them into your story completely before conducting the taste test. Then listen to them groan in disgust!

TIP!

For a holiday flare, use dried cranberries in sparkling cider!

21

WHAT IS GAS?

Gas is made from the air we swallow and the gases produced during digestion.

Some people call it passing gas. Others call it farting, tooting, breaking wind, or barking spiders. But it all means the same thing. Gas bubbles move from inside to outside of our bodies. Some farts are silent and smelly, while some are shockingly loud and odorless. Gas made from swallowed air is mostly made up of nitrogen and carbon dioxide, which produces large, relatively odorless air bubbles. Gas made from bacterial fermentation in our digestive system produces small, smelly air bubbles (Hydrogen sulfide is the chemical guilty of that potent rotten-egg odor!). But the truth is, everyone toots!

GAS
(THE STINKY KIND)

JOY OF A GOOD
VIBRATION

22 STRANGE BUT TRUE!

Books written in medieval Europe and other historical documents make reference to *flatulists*, or performers hired to provide entertainment based on the creative, sometimes melodic, but undoubtedly funny pastime of passing gas. These flatulists were similar to the modern Canadian duo, Terrance and Phillip, on the TV show *South Park!*

23 MAKE THEM LAUGH!

Q: Why should you only put 239 beans in bean soup?
A: Because one more would make it too farty.

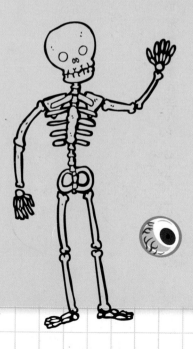

Q: Why did the skeleton burp?
A: Because he didn't have the guts to fart.

Q: What did one eyeball say to the other eyeball?
A: Between you and me, something smells.

DID YOU KNOW?

WASN'T ME!

24

The average person will pass gas 14 times a day, producing anywhere from 1 cup to a 1/2 gallon of gas!

FART AROUND!

25

Whoopee cushion farts
Blow up a whoopee cushion, then quickly deflate it with your hands or by sitting on it. For more fun, get someone to sit on the cushion without knowing!

26

Arm farts
Grab your underarm with the open palm of your opposite hand. Make sure to leave some space for air. Now flap your loose arm up and down to cut the cheese without the unpleasant odor.

NOISY FARTS

Long, long ago, in a time of kingdoms, mystery, and magic, there lived a little dragon named Fergus who was feared throughout the land.

What could possibly be so scary about a tiny dragon? His ferocious fumes!

WHAT YOU'LL NEED

Mixture A
- ¼ cup white glue
- Food coloring (any color)
- ¼ cup water
- 2 tablespoons cornstarch

Mixture B
- 4 teaspoons Borax*
- 1⅓ cup warm water
- Plastic bag or airtight container

HOW TO MAKE IT

Begin by mixing the glue with the food coloring. Once finished, blend water, the glue mixture, and cornstarch together. Set aside Mixture A. Mix the Borax and water until the Borax is dissolved to create Mixture B. Pour Mixture A into Mixture B. Do not stir; simply knead the flubbery substance in your hands. Store it in a plastic bag or an airtight container. When you want to make farting sounds, take it out of the plastic, and put it in an empty yogurt or pudding container. Plunge your fingers down into it, and pull them out to make wet, juicy farting sounds.

*Borax is a general cleaning agent. Care should be taken not to ingest or swallow.

28

WHAT IS POOP?

Poop is the waste produced during the final step of the digestive process.

Your average piece of poop is made up of mostly water—roughly 75 percent. The other 25 percent consists of dead bacteria from your intestines, fibrous matter, living bacteria, phosphates, mucus, dead cells, and proteins. Poop mainly smells because of sulfur contained in the organic compounds skatole, indole, and mercaptans, which are produced by bacteria. Humans dedicate so little time to discussing "the excretion of fecal matter, or pooping," but the truth is, it's a natural—and hopefully regular—part of our daily lives.

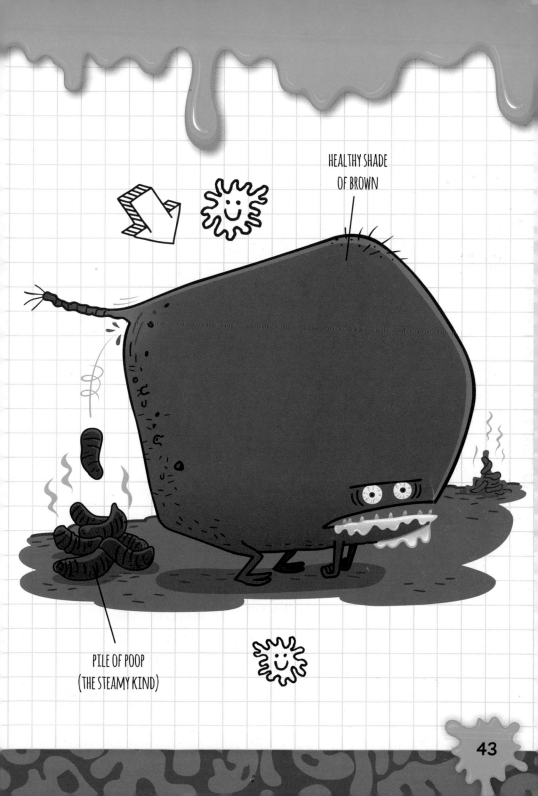

HEALTHY SHADE
OF BROWN

PILE OF POOP
(THE STEAMY KIND)

43

29 EXPAND YOUR VOCABULARY

Who knew animal poop could be called so many different things?

There's *bat guano, bird whitewash, buffalo chips, chimp chunks, cow pies, doggy doody, elk duds, horse apples, kitty bon bons, land mines, manure, meadow muffins, mouse pills, poodle patties, rabbit raisins,* and *scat.* What other words can you think of?

COWPIES

Manure   Buffalo chips   Horse APPLES

44

30 STRANGE BUT TRUE!

The Groom of the King's Close Stool was a promising position created in the 1500s to assist the king with his bowel movements. The "stool" referred to the portable commode that followed his royal highness at all times, along with water, towels, and a washbowl. The job of the groom included monitoring the diet of the king and collecting data that would determine the best schedule for his movements. The most shocking part? Besides the obvious poop factor! The position was well respected and often filled by the sons of noblemen, who were paid handsomely.

31 MAKE THEM LAUGH!

Q: Who goes to the bathroom in the middle of a party?
A: A party pooper!

Q: What is brown and sits on a piano bench?
A: Beethoven's last movement!

Q: How do you get out of an elephant's stomach?
A: Run around until you get pooped out.

32 POOP COLOR CHART

Because of stercobilin created as the bacteria in your intestine metabolizes bile from your gall bladder, poop is generally a lovely shade of brown. But if your poop's a different color, pay attention! It could mean something.

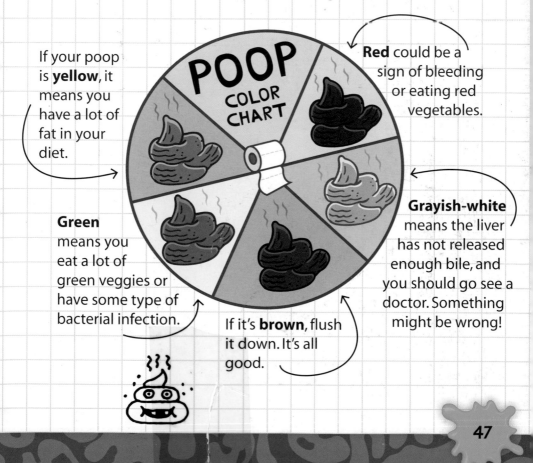

If your poop is **yellow**, it means you have a lot of fat in your diet.

Red could be a sign of bleeding or eating red vegetables.

Green means you eat a lot of green veggies or have some type of bacterial infection.

Grayish-white means the liver has not released enough bile, and you should go see a doctor. Something might be wrong!

If it's **brown**, flush it down. It's all good.

DID YOU KNOW?

33

I'M KING OF POOP MOUNTAIN!

Dung beetles burrow in poop, eat poop, lay their eggs in poop, and some even make perfectly round balls of it so they can roll it away with them. Their favorite poop is elephant poop. A single pile can weigh 5 pounds!

34 Many animals, including gorillas, rabbits, and dogs, can be found eating their poop. Rabbits eat lots of plants, so their poop contains quite a bit of undigested matter. Rabbits who eat their poop get more nutrients out of their food. Some animals produce vitamins from bacteria in their intestines that they wouldn't otherwise receive. Dogs, for example, find that poop can be a good source of protein, which is why they can sometimes be found nosing around in the litter box!

35

GROSS BUT NOT TRUE

ALIEN POOP

The Poop Patrol has one mission—to discover what doo-doo may lie (or float) across the planets.

Scooping up samples with stellar speed, the patrol from Uranus scours cities across the universe for any skid mark left behind. These samples are sent back to the space ship, where they are analyzed and used as fuel. The surplus is transported home. They leave no port-a-potty unturned in their quest!

WHAT YOU'LL NEED

Mixture A

- ⅓ cup or 6 tablespoons water
- 1 tablespoon dark corn syrup
- ½ teaspoon white vinegar
- 1 tablespoon coffee grounds
- 4 drops of red food coloring
- 9 drops of green food coloring

Mixture B

- ½ cup cornstarch
- ⅓ cup or 6 tablespoons cold water

HOW TO MAKE IT

Combine and heat Mixture A in a small saucepan over medium heat. Bring to a boil. Combine Mixture B in a small bowl until blended. While stirring, add Mixture B into Mixture A. Keep stirring, and a dough-like mass will quickly develop. Remove from heat and let cool. Once cool enough to touch, shape the mixture into the desired poop size and shape. Let it cool completely.

NOW, WHAT DO YOU DO WITH IT?

- Leave a trail of fake poop, and don't tell anyone about it. Sit back, and watch people's reactions when they find the poop and try to clean it up.
- Shape the fake poop into Xs and Os, and play poop tic-tac-toe with it.
- Float the poop in a swimming pool without anyone noticing. Watch as chaos ensues.

36

WHAT IS BLOOD?

Blood is a super important bodily fluid that carries oxygen and nutrients to cells, transports metabolic waste products away from cells, and regulates body temperature.

Blood contains a clear liquid called *plasma*, as well as red blood cells, white blood cells, and platelets. Blood cells originate from stem cells located in spongy tissue, called *bone marrow*. Red blood cells contain iron-rich hemoglobin, without which we wouldn't receive enough oxygen to survive. White blood cells prevent disease and infections, and platelets allow blood to clot.

Humanity has always had a fascination with blood and the folklore surrounding it—especially the vampire Dracula. The "real" Dracula who inspired Bram Stoker's story was a 15th century Romanian ruler, Vlad III, better known today by his nickname, "Vlad the Impaler." Old Vlad was known for being cruel on the battlefield and was even rumored to dip bread in the blood of his victims before eating it!

FLOWS FROM HEAD TO TOE

PLASMA PLATELET PUNCH

RICH IRON FLAVOR

37 STRANGE BUT TRUE!

George Washington, the first president of the United States, retired to his home at Mount Vernon to live out the rest of his life as a quiet farmer. In December of 1799, Washington spent a day riding on horseback through the snow. The next morning, he awoke severely ill and called for his doctor.

Bloodletting, a common medical practice at the time, was believed to prevent or cure disease and illness. It was practiced for over 2,000 years. Washington reportedly encouraged this treatment, so his doctor drew blood at least four times that day, adding up to an estimated 2.4 liters. The average human body contains approximately 5 liters of blood. Many believe he was bled to death!

38 MAKE THEM LAUGH!

Q: Did you hear about the two blood cells?
A: They loved in vein.

Q: Why doesn't Dracula have friends?
A: Because he's a pain in the neck.

DID YOU KNOW?

39 Leeches have been used in the medical practice of bloodletting for centuries. A leech attaches itself to a person's skin, bites down with its sharp teeth, and sucks up as much as 5 to 10 milliliters of blood—that's almost 10 times its own weight!

40

The human body makes two million new red blood cells per second and contains a total of 20 to 30 trillion red blood cells at any given moment in time!

41

All blood isn't red. Crabs have blue blood; some earthworms have green blood; and many invertebrates, like starfish, have clear or yellowish blood.

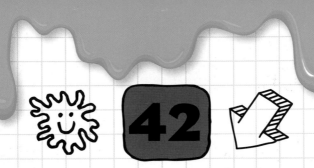

REALLY GROSS SCABS

GROSS BUT NOT TRUE

This disgusting freak of nature lives in rivers and lakes, where it feeds on fish and tadpoles.

After each meal, it sheds its grotesque skin, leaving a trail of scabs and who knows what else along the water's edge. It's so revolting that no one has bothered to learn much about where it came from or what it wants. Is the scabenger creature scary? Is it shy and misunderstood? Who knows and who cares? It's repulsive! Flake off!

NATURE'S BAND-AID

A *scab* is a layer of dried blood that protects cells underneath it as they repair themselves.

58

WHAT YOU'LL NEED

Fake Blood
- 1 tablespoon corn syrup
- 15 drops red food coloring
- 1 drop blue food coloring
- 1 tablespoon cornstarch

Fake Scabs
- Cornflakes or branflakes
- Corn syrup
- Fake blood or red makeup
- Cotton swab

HOW TO MAKE IT

For fake blood, mix the corn syrup and food coloring in a bowl. Add the cornstarch, and mix again. Store in the refrigerator. (It keeps for only a couple of days.)

To make your scabs, crush a branflake or a cornflake, and stick the pieces on your skin using a tiny dab of corn syrup. Let them dry, and then color the area around the flakes with a cotton swab dipped in fake blood. Be warned, the food coloring in this recipe washes off skin with soap and water, but it will stain clothing.

TIP!

A piece of puffed rice makes a very realistic wart. Try it!

43

WHAT IS MEDICINE?

Medicine is a big term that includes diagnosing, treating, and preventing diseases or other things that lead to humans being unhealthy.

Preventative medicine is why you are forced to visit the dentist regularly and eat a healthy diet—doctors use data-driven science to keep you running your very best! Medicine also includes adaptive or assistive technologies like a new pair of eyeglasses or a wheelchair that allows you to zoom faster than your able-bodied friends!

Curative medicine can include exploring DNA to find cures for diseases or performing cutting-edge surgeries. And then, of course, there's the actual medicine, also known as the nasty stuff your parents give you when you are feeling crummy. So how can medicine possibly be gross? Let's walk down that disgusting path together.

SICKLY GRAY
SKIN

CAUTION:
NASTY MEDICINE

CONTAMINATED CONTAINER

61

44 STRANGE BUT TRUE!

Thousands of years ago, people used the medical practice of *trephination*, which involves drilling a hole (sometimes several) into the skull to cure illness. Automatic drills hadn't been invented yet, so the holes were created very slowly. The practice was used to treat headaches, toothaches, seizures, blood clots, and mental illness. Many ancient skulls show humans survived the treatment and even had it performed on multiple occasions. Some cultures even used the practice for non-medical purposes, like ridding the body of evil spirits.

45 MAKE THEM LAUGH!

Q: What did the patient who swallowed money say to the X-ray technician?
A: Do you see any change in me?

Q: Why did the cookie go to the hospital?
A: He felt crummy!

Q: What did the judge say to the dentist?
A: Do you swear to pull the tooth, the whole tooth, and nothing but the tooth?

Q: When is the best time to go to the dentist?
A: Tooth-hurty.

DID YOU KNOW?

46 According to the Ebers Papyrus (an ancient Egyptian document of herbal knowledge written around 1500 BCE), donkey, fly, gazelle, and dog poop was a popular remedy for various ailments. Despite the diseases that could be transmitted in the process, it may have been effective. Research shows some bacteria in animal dung contains antibiotics.

 **47** *Helminthic therapy* uses intestinal worms to alleviate medical conditions such as allergies and inflammatory bowel disease. A protective response is triggered when parasites invade the body. It allows a person to survive the parasite and minimizes the damage it causes. Supporters of helminthic therapy believe that industrialized societies have become too clean, eradicating organisms our bodies need. The problem? Worms can only enter the body if you swallow them or let them crawl through your skin.

URINE GELATIN CUPS

A urine culture is a routine medical test for kids and adults. Your doctor hands you a sterile cup and asks you to urinate in it. The test usually doesn't happen at home!

THE SCIENCE

Doctors test urine for germs (mainly bacteria) that exceed normal levels and may cause an infection in the urinary tract. About 95 percent of urine is made up of water; if no other liquid is available, urine can be safe to drink!

HOW TO MAKE IT

Don't worry! You don't need a doctor or any real urine for this activity. Armed with your knowledge of urine cultures and the makeup of pee, you're ready to freak out your friends with this suspiciously pee-like drink! Follow the directions on the back of the packaging to make a batch of gelatin. While still in liquid form, pour the gelatin into the specimen cups, and set them in the refrigerator to cool and settle. Make sure to leave one specimen cup empty, and set it aside.

WHAT YOU'LL NEED

- Specimen cups with lids (found at your local drug store or online)
- Package of lemon-flavored gelatin

When a friend visits, set the empty cup out on the bathroom counter and hide a gelatin-filled cup in a place your friend won't be able to see it. Make sure they've noticed the empty cup and are eyeing it questioningly as you enter the bathroom. Now flush the toilet, ditch the empty cup, and grab the prefilled one before leaving, making sure to make as much noise as possible to get their attention. When you are sure they are looking, pop the top off the specimen cup ever so casually, and gulp it down! If anyone asks, remind them urine is mostly made of water.

49

WHAT ARE CREEPY, CRAWLY CREATURES?

There are over a million different animal species on our lovely planet! Some creep. Some crawl. They all move, eat, breathe, and excrete waste (aka poop!).

Some animals are used for food, medicine, and clothing. Bees keep plants growing through pollination, and bats reduce the need for insecticide. But for all of their wonderful qualities, some of these creatures can be downright gross! Take houseflies, for example. Flies find any type of decaying human or animal waste to be a highly attractive meal. They spit their saliva onto their food, and use their mouths like a straw to suck up their snack in liquid form.

DIGESTIVE SALIVA

ROTTEN PIECE OF MEAT

50 STRANGE BUT TRUE!

Jackals are members of the canine family, and they live primarily in Africa, Asia, and Southeast Europe. They are considered opportunistic omnivores, meaning they aren't terribly picky eaters. Some of their favorite meals consist of large birds, poisonous snakes, and reptiles. However, they are most popularly known as part of the "clean-up crew." After a lion or tiger has killed an animal and taken what they want, jackals move in, even if the animal has been rotting for days. To feed their pups, jackals simply trot on home and regurgitate. So next time your parent asks you if you are hungry, make sure to find out what's on the menu.

51 MAKE THEM LAUGH!

Q: Why did the cow cross the road?
A: To get to the udder side!

Q: Why do fish live in salt water?
A: Because pepper makes them sneeze!

Q: How does a frog feel when it has a broken leg?
A: Unhoppy!

DID YOU KNOW?

I LOVE SLURPEES!

52

Tarantulas—large, hairy arachnids— secrete digestive enzymes that turn their prey into liquid and slurp up what's left of them.

53 Some sea cucumbers can poop out their internal organs as a defense mechanism. These organs trick their predators, and within a few weeks, the sea cucumber is able to regenerate them! Creepy, huh?

GREASY GRIMY GOPHER GUTS

Gross songs that make grown-ups grimace are a time-honored tradition around the campfire or on the school bus. That shy but famous writer Anonymous gets all the credit for this one.

Great green gobs of greasy grimy gopher guts, mutilated monkey meat, little birdies' dirty feet. Sounds yummy, let's eat!
—Anonymous

- Green gelatin
- Gummy worms

HOW TO MAKE IT

Use either ready-made green gelatin or have a parent help you make it from boxed gelatin. Mix prepared gelatin with gummy worms, making sure to stir it up with a spoon so it looks chunky and slimy.

55

MUTILATED MONKEY MEAT

WITH LITTLE BIRDIES' DIRTY FEET

WHAT YOU'LL NEED

- Chocolate pudding
- Tapioca pudding
- Red licorice strings
- Broken pretzel sticks

HOW TO MAKE IT

Combine equal portions of chocolate and tapioca pudding. Add the licorice strings, and mix well. Sprinkle your concoction with broken pretzels.

NO GUTS, NO GLORY

As gross as these recipes sound, they actually taste
A. Really, really bad
B. Not half bad
C. Surprisingly good
(The correct answer is C—if you're starving!)

56

CREEPY CRAWLY CAKE

There may not be an example of a more profound slice of creepy crawly heaven than this culinary delight!

Who doesn't enjoy a cake filled with bugs? The more scrumptious looking the cake is, the more horrified your guests will be! Delish!

WHAT YOU'LL NEED

- Layered cake and frosting
- Plastic toy bugs and insects

You can purchase plastic bugs and insects at your local party supply store. Make sure to wash them with soap and water before using!

HOW TO MAKE IT

There are two ways you can go about this, and the first is to buy cake mix from your local grocery store (or if you're a master in the kitchen, bake a cake from scratch). The second way to do this (if time is not on your side) is to buy a premade cake from your local bakery. The cake works best if it is tall and layered, so you may need to make or buy frosting as well.

Before covering the cake in frosting, flip the bottom side up. Cut a cone out of the center and remove it, being careful not to cut through the top of the cake. Once finished, cut a slice of cake off the top of the cone, place your plastic creepy crawlies inside the cake, and gently put the bottom of the cone back. Use a little frosting to seal it. Finally, flip the cake over, and cover it with frosting.

When it's time to serve dessert, enjoy all the moaning and groaning you hear when you cut into it. Make sure to look outraged. For extra fun, have an unsuspecting adult cut into it, and while the grossness settles, act none the wiser. "Who, me? Why I'd never!"

57

INEDIBLE MAGGOTS

Who doesn't gag just a bit when they think of, let alone see, a maggot or two?

THE SCIENCE

Maggots are the larvae (aka babies) of flies. Though these squirming bundles of joy are the opposite of adorable, they play many important roles in society. Fishermen use them as bait, and medical practitioners have used them for ages to help clean wounds, as the maggots enjoy a tasty snack of dead tissue, leaving healthy tissue behind and aiding the healing process. Of course, maggots can often be found chowing down near rotten food and garbage.

WHAT YOU'LL NEED

- Bottle of clear latex (from your local costume supply store)
- White acrylic paint
- Black permanent marker (or black acrylic paint)
- Scissors
- A clean, glass surface
- Blow dryer (optional)

HOW TO MAKE IT

Place a drop of latex on the glass surface, and spread into a circle that's approximately ½" in diameter. Don't get too fussy with it. The size doesn't have to be exact! Make as many maggots as you like, and leave them to dry. If you are as impatient as I can be, blast them with a blow dryer to speed up the process.

Once dry (they will be clear), grab the white acrylic paint, and apply a quick coat of paint over the tops. Don't worry if the paint touches the glass, it will wipe off quite easily at the end! Once the paint is dry, pick one circle to start with. Gently roll one side, making it look like a little white burrito. Pinch it a bit to give it the curly look of a real maggot. Once you've done this for each circle, snip one end off, and apply either black acrylic paint or a black sharpie. Go easy on the black. You want it to look like the small and subtle head of the critter. You can also trim down the opposite end to give it a slightly pointy tail. Finally, carefully place the maggots where they will disgust your friends!

58

WHAT IS BACTERIA?

They can be found in the ground, air, and water. You can even find them in radioactive waste, on spacecrafts, and all over the human body.

You can thank bacteria for cheese and yogurt. There are other helpful strains as well. *Escherichia coli*, for example, hangs out in the stomach and helps synthesize vitamin K, which encourages blood to clot when a person is wounded.

But there are some bacteria known as pathogens best never experienced. For example, *Bacillus anthracis* is naturally found in the soil as a dormant spore and only becomes an active growing cell when it's hanging out with sugars, waters, and other nutrients found in an animal's (or human's) body. It produces poisonous toxins and the deadly disease anthrax.

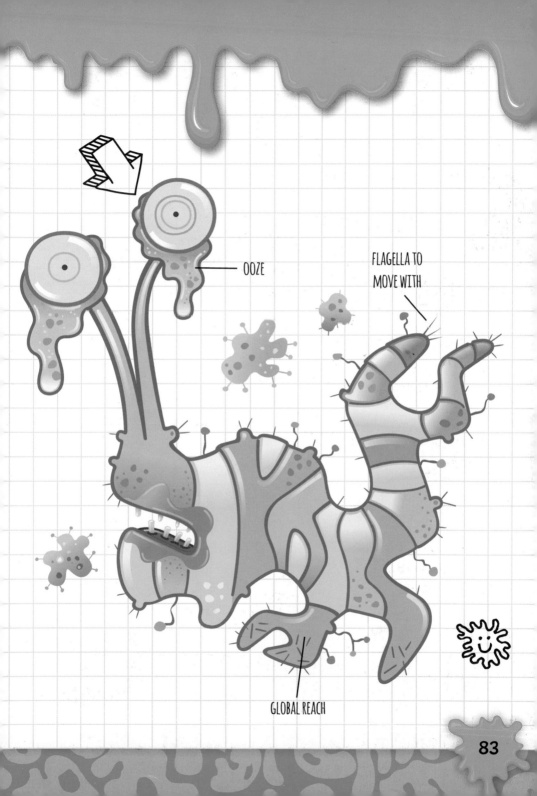

OOZE

FLAGELLA TO
MOVE WITH

GLOBAL REACH

59 STRANGE BUT TRUE!

During the American Civil War, and specifically the Battle of Shiloh, bacteria literally lit things up! After an especially violent battle, soldiers sat in the rain and mud waiting for help. As dusk fell, they noticed something weird—their wounds appeared to be glowing! The mysterious light was called "Angel's Glow" after it was discovered that the soldiers with the glowing wounds healed quicker and had a higher survival rate.

So what was going on? A bioluminescent bacteria called *Photorhabdus luminescens* was in the mud the soldiers sat in. The bacteria and the nematodes, or worms, it lives in waged their own microbial civil war to create a chemical cocktail that destroyed the competition. The nematodes helped the soldiers they infected by killing pathogens that would have caused serious infections. Positively illuminating!

 # 60 MAKE THEM LAUGH!

Q: What is the only thing worse than a mecium?
A: A paramecium.

Q: What did one bacteria say to the other bacteria?
A: Let's make like an amoeba and split.

Q: Why did the microbe cross the road?
A: He was stuck to the chicken's butt.

Q: Why did the bacteria cross the playground?
A: To get to the other slide.

DID YOU KNOW?

61

There are more bacteria in your mouth than people in the world. In fact, between 10 million and 1 billion bacteria get exchanged when two people kiss each other. Ewwwwww!

62

When you flush a toilet, the germs inside the bowl can travel up to 6 feet and linger in the air for up to 2 hours. These germs can land on your toothbrush if it has been left out. They can also be inhaled or attach themselves to your clothing, keeping you company throughout the day.

63

If you've ever eaten beans and gotten gas, you can thank bacteria! Beans carry a type of sugar called *oligosaccharides*, which is hard for bacteria to break down, causing them to release gas. So you can blame that bacteria for your flatulence, but just remember, whoever denied it supplied it.

FARM THE BACTERIA

This fun but fairly gross experiment is done regularly in labs all around the world. You can use it to finally prove your sibling's bedroom is dirtier than yours.

THE SCIENCE

When doing this experiment in the lab, scientists take care to label their petri dishes. They mark where, when, and how the sample was collected. Keeping a clear record in the beginning helps them make observations and draw conclusions once the creepy crawlies start to grow.

WHAT YOU'LL NEED

- 200 ml boiling water
- 4 teaspoons agar
- 3 teaspoons white sugar
- 2 teaspoons bouillon
- Petri dishes
- Cotton swabs

TIP!

You can purchase inexpensive petri dishes online or substitute them with deli containers, but make sure they can tolerate super hot water. Agar can be found online and at most Asian grocery stores.

HOW TO MAKE IT

Divide and label the petri dishes. Boil water, remove from heat, and stir in the agar until it's completely dissolved. Bring the water back up to a boil, add sugar and bouillon, and stir it up like you have never stirred before! Pour the mixture into the petri dishes, filling them to about ¼". Put the lids on, and place the dishes in the refrigerator to cool. Now you're ready to gather your cultures!

Using a new cotton swab for each item, swab the inside of your mouth, the toilet seat, doorknobs, the family computer, the trashcan, and even your pet's armpit. Rub the swab on the inside of each petri dish, and quickly replace the lids to prevent anything else from getting inside! Store the dishes in a warm area so the bacteria will grow. Consider taping down the lids to keep any curious, fellow grossologists away.

Write down your observations as the creepy crawlies grow! You may end up with a dish of fungi, mold, or bacteria, each one its own variety of shapes and colors.

65

WHAT ARE ZOMBIES?

Zombies are the fictional walking dead that have been reanimated into violent people-eaters.

Zombies in modern-day storytelling are the result of a pandemic started by a contagion. The contagion is generally transmitted through the air or from a bug bite. The result is not terribly bright, lumbering, angry, super-hungry former humans. Even though zombies don't exist, some scientists have discovered a pathway in humans for a virus that could result in zombie-like behavior. It requires the virus to travel through the olfactory nerve, which we use to smell with, and attack the brain, while leaving the rest of our bodies intact. But no one is freaking out yet.

DECAYING
SKIN

APPETITE FOR
BRAINS

AWKWARD, STIFF
STEPS

91

66 YOU MIGHT BE A ZOMBIE

IF YOU SUFFER FROM...

Impulse Control

Zombies aren't terribly bright and don't seem to think through life-or-death decisions. This indicates frontal lobe damage, changing the very essence of their human personality into an uncontrollable monster (assuming they weren't already one, that is).

Constant Shuffling

Zombies have a lumbering, awkward gait. It's highly likely their lack of balance is the result of damage to their *cerebellum*, which is the part of the brain that helps living humans with coordination and motor skills.

Anger

Zombies are mean, hyperaggressive biters, which is likely caused by damage to the anterior cingulate cortex. This part of the brain works in tandem with *amygdalae*, a pair of almond-shaped regions deep inside the brain responsible for base emotions like rage. Normally the frontal lobe keeps them in check, but if it's been damaged, there is nothing to counteract the crazy.

Insatiable Hunger

Zombies truly give the term hangry a new meaning. No matter how much (or how many brains) they eat, they are still hungry, pointing to a damaged hypothalamus. Your *hypothalamus* tells you when your stomach's full, but zombies' hypothalamuses don't work properly, which causes a condition known as *hyperphagia*. So they keep eating, never having to worry about their decaying figure.

THE ZOMBIE SURVIVAL KIT

How can one avoid being turned into a zombie in the event of a zombie apocalypse?

The United States Center for Disease Control and Prevention has come up with a list of preparedness items and a plan in the event that a zombie apocalypse seems imminent. (Or some other, more boring, emergency, like a hurricane, earthquake, or other natural disaster.)

WHAT YOU'LL NEED

- Water (1 gallon per person, per day)
- Food (stock up on non-perishable items that you eat regularly)
- Medications (including prescription and non-prescription meds)
- Tools and supplies (utility knife, duct tape, battery-powered radio, etc.)
- Sanitation and hygiene (household bleach, soap, towels, etc.)
- Clothing and bedding (a change of clothes for each family member and blankets)
- Important documents (copies of your driver's license, passport, and birth certificate to name a few)
- First-aid supplies (although you're a goner if a zombie bites you, you can use these supplies to treat basic cuts and lacerations you might get)

Once you've made your Zombie Survival Kit, you should sit down with your family and come up with a plan for where you would go and who you would call if zombies started appearing outside your doorstep:

- Pick a meeting place for your family to regroup.

- Make a list of local contacts like the police, fire department, and your local zombie-response team.

- Plan your evacuation route. When zombies are hungry, they won't stop until they get food (i.e., brains), which means you need to get out of town fast!

68 STRANGE BUT TRUE!

Taphophobia is the fear of being buried alive. Modern medicine makes it difficult for such an event to happen, but in the 19th century, doctors realized that the lack of medical advances likely meant people had been buried alive (or at the very least, not *quite* dead).

Ambitious inventors patented "safety coffins" in order to alleviate the public's anxieties. In many cases, a string was placed in the body's hand or tied around the wrist, so that if moved, a red flag would wave or a bell would ring and alert those above ground that they were still alive.

69 MAKE THEM LAUGH!

Q: When do zombies go to sleep?
A: When they are dead tired.

Q: Why did the zombie lose the lawsuit?
A: He had no leg to stand on.

Q: Do zombies eat popcorn with their fingers?
A: No, they eat their fingers separately.

Q: What did the vegetarian say when he turned into a zombie?
A: GRAAAAAAAAIIIIIIIINNNNNNNNS!!!!

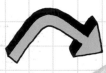

DID YOU KNOW?

I'LL DRINK TO THAT!

70

Skulls of the dead were used as drinking cups and trophies in ancient Europe and Asia. Cheers!

71

As recently as the 1800s, dentures were commonly made from teeth pulled from the mouths of dead soldiers.

72

In ancient Europe and Asia, grave digging was commonly performed to create medicine made from human bones, blood, and fat. Royalty, priests, and scientists believed the medicine would cure a whole host of ailments, ranging from seizures to headaches.

BAKED ZOMBIE INTESTINES

The next few pages contain some zombie-inspired recipes for you to feast upon during those occasions when you're hankering for a savory piece of intestines, a plump finger, or a gooey eyeball to chew on.
Make a dish to celebrate your most beloved spooky holiday, or just to liven up a boring evening!

WHAT YOU'LL NEED

- 1 package puff pastry
- Choice of filling (sausage, mushrooms, squash, or other tasty treats)
- 1 egg, beaten
- Food coloring
- Kitchen brush
- Parchment paper
- Scissors
- Baking sheet

HOW TO MAKE IT

Preheat the oven to 375° F, and line a baking sheet with parchment paper. Cut the pastry into long rectangular strips, and join them together to form a long strip of dough. Use pressure to keep the edges together but don't stress too much. You can arrange things the way you'd like them when you pour your guts out into the baking dish!

Spread your filling down the center of the dough, leaving a bit of space on each side to pinch close. Brush the edges with some egg, and pinch the whole thing shut. Carefully lift the pastry onto the baking sheet, and shape it until it looks like intestines, rolling it over so the pinched edge is on the bottom. Brush the whole thing with egg.

Dip your brush into some red food coloring (add a little blue for a darker color), and paint on the "blood."

74 SNOT-FILLED EYEBALLS

WHAT YOU'LL NEED

- Large marshmallows
- Candy-coated chocolate pieces (M&Ms)
- Mini-chocolate chips
- Tube of chocolate frosting or gel
- Tube of red decorating gel

HOW TO MAKE IT

Squish a candy-coated chocolate into your marshmallow to start your eyeball. Squirt a little chocolate frosting onto a mini chocolate chip and attach to the M&M. Complete by squiggling red gel to make bloodshot veins.

75 FRANK FINGERS

HOW TO MAKE IT

Microwave your hot dogs to make sure they are ready to eat. The easiest way? Plop them into a bun, place the whole thing into a paper towel, and tuck the sides of the paper towel around it.

Microwave the hot dog for 20 seconds, take it out, and carve out fingernails and slices for knuckles and joints. Pop the hot dog back in the microwave for 20 to 30 seconds, go crazy with the ketchup for the perfect bloody effect, and eat up!

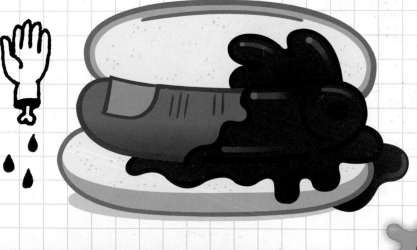

76

WHAT IS FOOD?

We usually think of food as yummy stuff that we daydream about, celebrate important milestones with, and get crabby without.

Our bodies need food and the nourishment it provides to function properly and stay healthy. Foods like grains and beans contain carbohydrates that our bodies break down into sugar. We turn that sugar, as well as fat, into energy. Foods like meat and eggs contain protein that our bodies use to build new cells, especially muscles.

The food people eat varies drastically around the world. To you, eating insects might be strange, but to over 2 billion people on our planet, eating insects is yummy! (Insects actually have more protein than fish or beef!) The way we eat has also changed over time.

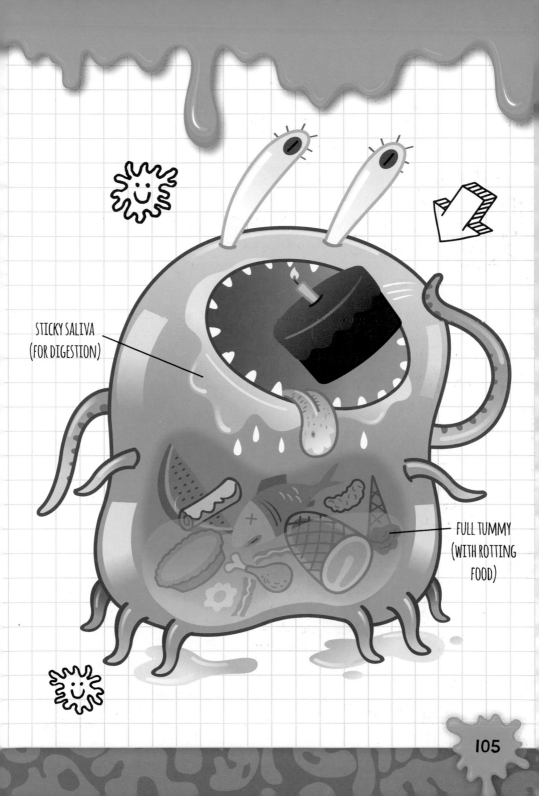

STICKY SALIVA
(FOR DIGESTION)

FULL TUMMY
(WITH ROTTING
FOOD)

77 STRANGE BUT TRUE!

Like many of life's greatest pleasures, food can be a little gross. Take garum, a fermented fish sauce, for example. (Please, take it.) Made from a mixture of fish intestines and blood, salt, and herbs left in the sun for up to three months, garum was extremely popular among

GARUM-YUM!

ancient Romans. The production of the paste was a major part of the economy in cities such as Pompeii. The fermenting garum smelled so bad that people were only allowed to make it outside the cities. While perhaps strange for a modern palate, Romans put garum on everything—meat, eggs, and even dessert!

78 MAKE THEM LAUGH!

Q: What do you call a fish without an eye?
A: Fsh!

Q: What's the difference between a fish and a piano?
A: You can't tuna fish.

Q: What do you get from a pampered cow?
A: Spoiled milk.

DID YOU KNOW?

79

Shellac, the hard glaze that coats jelly beans, is produced from tube-like secretions from lac insects.

80

Some of the vanilla flavoring in candies and baked goods is made from *castoreum*, a secretion from the anal glands of beavers.

TASTES GOOD TO ME!

81

In the 1800s, ketchup was used to treat diarrhea. Think about that the next time you dip your french fry in it.

RUBBER EGGS & CHICKEN BONES

CROSS BUT NOT TRUE

The goose may have laid golden eggs, but have you heard the one about the chicken that laid rubber eggs?

Didn't think so. Rancher Ralph in Roswell, New Mexico, noticed his chickens walking wobbly after UFOs flew over the chicken coop. He went to gather some eggs for breakfast, and they were so rubbery they bounced!

That night as Rancher Ralph dined on some of the tenderest chicken he'd ever eaten, he noticed the bones were like bendable rubber. "That's one crazy chicken," he said, patting his full stomach. Pollo loco, indeed!

HOW TO MAKE IT

Place an egg in a clear glass, and cover the egg with vinegar. Let it sit overnight, and observe the results. The longer the egg is left in vinegar, the more transparent it will become. Be extra careful when handling a raw egg—they can be awfully stinky if they break. Next try leaving a hard-boiled egg in vinegar for two nights. The shell magically disappears! Next time you eat fried chicken, save a leg or wing bone, and put it in vinegar. The bone will take about a week to get rubbery, but the results are very cool!

WHAT YOU'LL NEED

- Eggs
- Chicken bones
- White vinegar

THE SCIENCE

Vinegar is an acid that dissolves the calcium in the eggshell and the bone. That's the reason this egg-cellent experiment works.

NOW, WHAT DO YOU DO WITH THEM?

- Astound your friends.
- Ponder which came first: the chicken or the egg?
- If your egg is hard-boiled, see how high it can bounce.
- Put a flashlight behind it, and see if you can see through it.

83

MONSTER DISH

A monstrous dish is simply the best of both worlds, and when made correctly, it is quite yummy too!

This monster dish consists of one of the world's favorite meals—cooked rice. While it's suitably gross looking, the food will not go to waste. An epic win for all!

WHAT YOU'LL NEED

- Cooked rice
- Hard-boiled egg
- Cooked egg whites
- Black olives
- Red pepper
- Spam
- Seaweed
- Mint
- Feta cheese
- Serving dish

HOW TO MAKE IT

After cooking the rice, pour it into a serving dish. Layer the other ingredients on top of the rice, forming a spooky face. Use hard-boiled eggs for eyes and a slice of black olive for pupils. Place the slices of red pepper where your monster's mouth should be. Use chunks of egg whites for teeth and a piece of spam for a tongue. Create a wild hairstyle with seaweed, and sprinkle mint and feta on top. Now take a step back, and try not to scream.

NOW, WHAT DO YOU DO WITH IT?

Invite your friends over for a Gross Not Grand party. Pair your Monster Dish with the Frank Fingers from page 103. And if the shock on their faces doesn't satisfy you, get creative with even more gross dishes. What kind of nasty concoction can you create with a little spaghetti and some sausages? If this book has taught you anything, there's no level of grossness that can't be topped!

84

WHAT'S WITH ALL THAT BODY STUFF?

Humans may try to cover their gross innards with colorful clothes and polite manners. But under those layers, we're all the same: filled with pus, blood, snot, and all the ooey, gooey organs that make us work.

Our bodies are always changing, digesting, and yes, secreting. We're covered in hair, and our skin produces oils and odors that may be better left unmentioned. If you already know your boogers from your bones, read on to learn more about the parts of the human body that are harder to see. As you'll find out in this section, our bodies are just plain gross. The good news is that's exactly what makes us human.

PLUMP PIMPLES

SWEATY PITS

SMELLY FEET

85 STRANGE BUT TRUE!

In 2013, scientists from Trinity College in Dublin launched an exhibit that included cheeses made from the cells of human bodies. Lovely little microbes found in human mouths, toes, noses, belly buttons, and even tears were collected for these unique delicacies! The microbes were grown on various cheese rinds, and there you have it—cheeses that smell and taste like the body odors of the people providing the bacteria. So why on earth did the scientists decide to create human-bacteria cheese? They wanted to start a conversation about the similarities and differences between bacteria from the human body and bacteria in food, like cheese, that is ingested regularly.

86 MAKE THEM LAUGH!

Q: What did the belly button say just before it left?
A: I'm outtie here!

Q: What do body odor and peaches have in common?
A: They both grow around pits.

Q: What do you call cheese that's not yours?
A: Nacho cheese.

Q: Did you pick your nose?
A: No, I was born with it!

Q: What kind of flower grows on your face?
A: Tulips!

DID YOU KNOW?

87

Body odor is not the result of sweat. All by its lonesome, sweat is water generated by your body to cool off. It's those lovely bacteria that hang out in warm, sweaty places that cause the smell. While there's no "cure," there is deodorant. Make it your friend.

88

Demodex folliculorum, commonly referred to as *mites,* live on your eyelashes, eyebrows, in the folds of your nose, and pretty much everywhere else on your face. These little creatures live for an average of 18 to 24 days. During the day, they feed on dead skin cells in hair follicles, and at night, they come out and mate, laying up to 24 eggs in a single hair follicle! Geeze. Can you keep it down? We're trying to sleep here.

BUTTERSCOTCH EAR SWABS

People use cotton swabs—and occasionally their fingers—to rid their ears of wax.

The ear swabs in this activity are a disgusting little snack that pair well with the Urine Gelatin Cups on page 66.

THE SCIENCE

Earwax, or cerumen, is produced in the outer ear canal before slowly making its way to the opening of the ear. Its job is to moisturize skin and trap dirt before it can reach your sensitive eardrums and potentially cause infection.

WHAT YOU'LL NEED

- Butterscotch morsels
- Mini marshmallows
- Lollipop sticks (found at your local grocery store)
- Wax paper
- Small, microwavable dish

HOW TO MAKE IT

Begin by melting the butterscotch morsels in the microwave. Attach a mini marshmallow to each end of a lollipop stick.

TIP!

You could also use a double boiler on the stove to melt the butterscotch—whichever is more convenient!

Once the morsels are melted, grab a stick and swish the marshmallows around in the butterscotch. Set the dipped sticks on a piece of wax paper to dry (it's not recommended to cool these in the refrigerator, as they will harden and lose their realistic appearance), and ta da! You have a "fresh" ear swab. Yummy!

90

WHAT IS A BATHROOM?

If you ask most people what the grossest room in the house is, they normally vote for the bathroom.

Ancient people did their business in chamber pots that were dumped onto the streets when full. Ancient Greeks used stones as toilet paper, while the Romans used a sponge attached to a stick.

Chamber pots, along with outhouses or holes in the ground, were used for many years, but inevitably emptied into yards or sewers, ending up in local bodies of water. Queen Elizabeth I's godson, Sir John Harington, created Britain's first flush toilet in 1596, and water closets—early versions of the modern bathroom—first showed up in the 1700s. But modern toilet paper was still a long way off. Using old catalogs, newspapers, grass, water, hands, and even corncobs was the norm until the late 1800s when toilet paper was introduced. Even as recently as 1935, a large manufacturer advertised its toilet paper as "splinter free." No wonder the bathroom got such a dirty reputation.

THE ROYAL TUSH
HAMMOCK

SUSPICIOUSLY WET

91 STRANGE BUT TRUE!

During a 1984 mission, the *Discovery* space shuttle's wastewater system failed. When functioning properly, the system releases human waste into space after an astronaut finishes his or her business. But on this particular mission, the urine formed a 30-pound icicle on the outside of the shuttle. Worried that the icicle would break on re-entry and damage the shuttle's heat shield, the astronauts set about finding a way to remove it.

They pointed the icicle towards the sun to melt it, and when that didn't work, they used the shuttle's robot arm to break it. While this worked, the crew was still left without a working wastewater system, and therefore no working toilet for the rest of their six-day mission. They were forced to go number one in the same bags reserved for number twos. The problem? There's no gravity in space, meaning any spilled liquids tend to spray everywhere. Gives a whole new meaning to the term *meteor shower*, eh?

92 MAKE THEM LAUGH!

Q: What is brown and sticky?
A: A stick.

Q: What did one toilet say to the other toilet?
A: You look flushed.

Q: Did you hear the story about the germ?
A: Never mind. I don't want it spread all over.

DID YOU KNOW?

93 While the average toilet seat has 50 bacteria per square inch, public restroom floors have about 2 million!

126

94 You count on the bathtub as the spot to get clean, but the drain area can contain up to 19,470 bacteria per square inch.

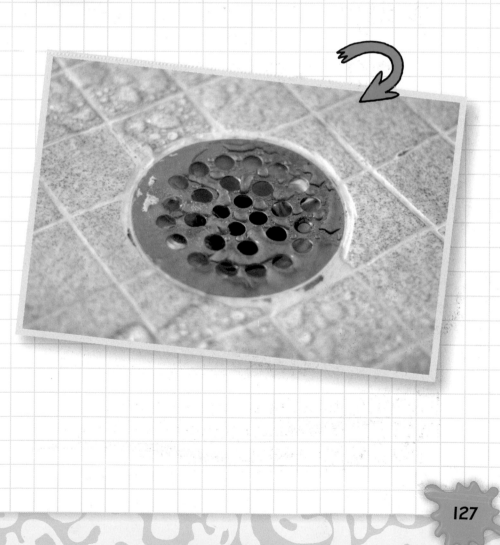

95

KITTY-LITTER FUDGE

By now, we know it's normal for some animals to root around the litter box, looking for a nutritious snack to munch on. But what about humans?

Armed with a little science, you can create some kitty litter fudge that will truly gross out your friends and family. With all eyes on you, pull a stringy piece of fudge from the litter box, dangle it over your mouth, and say yum! Smear some on your face for full effect.

THE SCIENCE

While the cat's poop might be a source of vitamins for animals, it's not recommended for human consumption. Cats and dairy animals often carry the parasite *Toxoplasma gondii* in their feces. Toxoplasmosis is a disease caused by the parasite. Most people never develop signs or symptoms, but babies born to infected mothers or people with weak immune systems can experience extremely serious complications.

WHAT YOU'LL NEED

- 3 cups sugar
- ¾ cups of butter or margarine
- 5 oz (small) can of evaporated milk (not sweetened condensed milk)
- 12 oz package of semi-sweet chocolate chips
- 7 oz jar of marshmallow cream
- 1 teaspoon vanilla
- Candy thermometer
- Brand new, unused litter tray and scoop
- One big box of puffed rice cereal
- Pre-buttered dish or cookie sheet

HOW TO MAKE IT

Make fudge by mixing butter, sugar, and evaporated milk in a 3-quart sauce pan. Stir as you go, and to prevent scorching, don't leave the pan alone for a second. Bring the mixture to a boil, and leave it for about 4 minutes or until your thermometer reaches 234° F when placed in the fudge. Remove the pan from the heat, and add the semi-sweet chocolate chips, marshmallow cream, and vanilla. Now stir, stir, stir!

Here's the tricky part—the fudge will initially be fairly thin, but as it cools, it will begin hardening. You will have a limited amount of time to transform your treat into a swirly piece of poop. Continue stirring until the fudge is still pourable, but holds its shape. Then pour some fudge into a plastic baggie, and snip off one corner to squeeze out those kitty poop shapes! Isn't it magical? (In a super gross way!) Make sure the pan you pour your shapes into is well-buttered, so the poops don't crack when taken out. Once cool, place them into the litter box with a whole lotta rice krispies. Now that's some delicious, delightful, and disgusting kitty-litter fudge!

TIP!

When you're stirring the fudge, pour some ice water into a second, larger container, and set the pan of fudge into it. Continue stirring so it will harden just a wee bit faster.

96

WHAT IS POLLUTION?

Unlike barf and snot, pollution isn't the cool kind of gross. It's just gross. Pollution is the process of making the environment unsafe, dirty, or unsuitable for use.

We can't always see or touch the contaminants that cause pollution. Sound, light, temperature, or chemicals—really anything that's artificial to the environment—can cause pollution. The effects can be devastating to local plant and animal life and, ultimately, to all humans.

Can pollution be reversed? Absolutely, but it will require education, time, and a ton of people working together to make it happen. So what can you do? The activities in this section will give you some great ideas on how to counteract the grossness, because the world outside your door shouldn't be another thing to gross out your friends with!

TOXIC
FUMES

HAZARDOUS
WASTE

ROTTEN FISH

97 STRANGE BUT TRUE!

In May 1953, Sir Edmund Hillary, the New Zealand mountaineer and explorer, was the first person to successfully reach the summit of Mt. Everest—the highest point on the Earth's surface. Until then, the mountain was pristine and relatively untouched by humans. Over the last 62 years, over 4,000 climbers have attempted the same trek, vastly changing the face of the mountain.

According to the Nepal Mountaineering Association, human waste and pollution have reached critical levels, threatening to spread disease on the 29,000 foot peak. The trails are filled with broken equipment, spent oxygen tanks, trash, and because humans go when they have to go, it has become a "fecal time bomb" threatening the watersheds at the lower elevations that depend on mountain water. To combat the pollution, local sherpas remove 26,500 pounds of human excrement each year, and the local government has started forcing hikers to bring 18 pounds of trash down with them. Scientists are even attempting to use solar panels to energize a "poop pit" that would break down human waste and provide energy to locals.

98 MAKE THEM LAUGH!

Q: Have you heard about the scientist who was obsessed with wind turbines?
A: She was a big fan.

Q: Have you heard the joke about the garbage truck?
A: Don't worry, it's a load of rubbish.

Q: What did the light say when it was turned off?
A: I'm delighted.

DID YOU KNOW?

99

The United States Environmental Protection Agency estimated in 2010 that Americans produce 4.3 pounds (1.95 kg) of waste per person each day, including furniture, clothing, food scraps, appliances, and more. Yeesh. Over half the waste ends up in landfills, and only 34 percent is recycled.

100 In 1347, the bubonic plague spread throughout Europe and wiped out nearly one-third of the population. The bacterium *Yersinia pestis* infects its host by invading the lymphatic system (a network that helps rid the body of infection). In London, pollution was rampant. People threw human waste into the streets and drank from contaminated water, and rats roamed freely. The fleas on these rodents easily carried the disease, and this, along with the unsanitary living conditions, helped spread the plague.

ANTI-GROSS GREEN ACTIVITIES

Anti-gross green activities are fun mini-projects you can do to help the world and be a leader in your family's efforts to lower its carbon footprint.

All of us have a carbon footprint, which is an estimate of the amount of greenhouse gases (gases that trap heat in the earth's atmosphere) we produce. The size of your footprint depends on: the energy used in your home, your form of transportation, and the waste you produce.

Don't worry—even if you aren't old enough to make these big life decisions, you can gently remind adults that there are always ways to live a greener life! Do it for your family (and future family), as well as Mother Earth. If you come up with ideas of your own, write them down. They could lead to a life-changing engineering or recycling project that can contribute to the greater good!

WHAT YOU CAN DO

- Compost your organic waste (animal and plant-based material) to reduce your use of pesticides, fertilizers, and water.

- Pester your family to turn the thermostat down a degree in the winter and up a degree in the summer. Adjusting the thermostat can reduce energy consumption by 10 percent or more!

- Reuse shopping bags, and avoid buying products that have tons of packaging (which requires a lot of energy to make).

- Drink tap water from a reusable bottle.

- Unplug all unused electronic devices. They consume energy whether they're being used or not.

- Microwave food whenever possible, instead of using the oven. It uses way less energy!

- Don't use more water than necessary. Turn off the tap while brushing your teeth, take shorter showers, and tell an adult if you notice a leaky faucet. A drop per second wastes around 2,400 gallons of water per year!

- Collect rainwater. Check out cool, inexpensive designs online, and get your family to join in!

- Be the light switch monitor. When someone leaves a room, make sure the lights are turned off!

- Make sure to donate your old clothes and toys to a local shelter or donation center, and discourage anyone in your family from throwing things they've outgrown into the trash.

- Be creative! Get out your favorite journal, start up the internet (to generate ideas), and gather your art supplies to start designing and decorating everyday household items that can be upcycled or recycled. For example, there are countless fun things to do with empty cereal boxes!

Remember: a curious mind is never a gross mind! So educate yourself about pollution, physics, chemistry, and biology. With a little science, you'll have everything you need to know how to make your audience say *ew* or *aw*!

GLOSSARY

Arachnid: A type of animal that has 8 legs and a body with 2 parts. Think spiders.

Bacteria: A teeny, tiny organism living in soil, water, or inside a living critter. Some are helpful, and some not so much.

Bioluminescent: The making and showing off of light by some living creature. Ever seen a firefly?

Carnivore: An animal that would rather eat your burger than your fries. A flesh-eater.

Concoction: A creation made from combining other things or an invention! This book is a concoction of grossness.

Contagion: A disease that moves through a population from one living thing to another. Think Zombies!

Culture: The uber fun growing of living stuff, usually in a jellylike nutrient!

Decaying: The decomposition, or breaking down of, living matter!

Enzymes: A complex protein that speeds up reactions without getting involved. (Think of a barbecue and lighter fluid. The lighter fluid is like an enzyme.)

Gelatin: A gummy or sticky protein substance made of a trio of amino acids. It's fun because it wiggles.

Germs: A microscopic critter that can cause diseases. This is why you wash your hands.

Herbivore: An animal that would rather eat your lettuce than your hamburger. A plant eater.

Infection: A disease caused by germs growing throughout an organism. Pinkeye is an example. Yeek.

Ingest: The act of taking something in for digestion. You. Me. Pizza.

Mechanism: A process that is responsible for some type of natural occurrence. Swallowing is the mechanism for digesting the pizza.

Microbe: A teeny, tiny organism that can only be seen with a microscope.

Mutilate: To destroy or severely alter a necessary part. Zombies enjoy this.

Omnivore: An animal that will eat either your burger, your fries, your salad, or your milkshake. A plant or animal eater.

Organs: A part of a creature that consists of cells and tissues and is specialized for a particular task. Your tongue is a muscular organ that helps with the task of eating pizza.

Pandemic: A disease that occurs over a wide area and affects a whole lot of people. Put on your sneakers and run.

Parasite: A living organism that lives in or on another living organism like the mites in your eyelashes.

Pathogen: These are bad. They are the germs that cause disease. Yuck.

Predator: An animal that stays alive by eating other animals.

Radioactive: The release of energy or particles from breaking apart atoms. The incredible Hulk anyone?

Recipes: Instructions for making things. This book is filled with gross ones.

Regenerate: To renew or be reborn.

Sedentary: Sitting or not moving much.

Sterile: Super clean without any microscopic critters.

Stimulation: To be made active. Like when you are ready to make gross, slimy stuff.

Tissue: An enclosed mass or layer of cells that make up the structures of a plant or animal.

Toxin: Substances created by a living creature designed to poison others.

Virus: A super tiny infectious agent that consists of DNA (or RNA) surrounded by a coat of protein. They vary in complexity, and are known to causes diseases. Nasty things can come in small packages.

Wound: An injury that involves breaking or cutting of bodily tissues.

ABOUT THE AUTHOR

Julie Huffman is a former high school chemistry teacher and current science specialist in her Southern California school district. She also teaches a science methods class at a local University. While attending the University of Nebraska Omaha, Julie worked at several informal science organizations learning all about the fun ways to teach sometimes challenging concepts to kids. After 14 years of working in the classroom, she's convinced that teaching is more fun than eating worms and is thrilled to have been chosen as a Los Angeles County Teacher of the Year. Julie and her daughter are also owners of a successful nerdy Etsy shop known as ShopGibberish.

The inspiration for this book came from her yucky husband, Wayne, and her two disgusting kids, Nicholas and Jenavieve. This book is dedicated to them and the gross kids she's worked with for the last 20 years. They have all taught her the real joy and meaning of attaining goals and making fun, and when possible, disgustingly gross education a priority.